Augmented Reality using Appcelerator Titanium Starter

Learn to create Augmented Reality applications in no time using the Appcelerator Titanium Framework

Trevor Ward

BIRMINGHAM - MUMBAI

Augmented Reality using Appcelerator Titanium Starter

First published: October 2012

Production Reference: 1191012

Published by Packt Publishing Ltd.
Livery Place
35 Livery Street
Birmingham B3 2PB, UK.

ISBN 978-1-84969-390-5

www.packtpub.com

Credits

Author
Trevor Ward

Reviewers
Ben Bahrenburg
Imraan Jhetam

Acquisition Editor
Kartikey Pandey

Commissioning Editor
Meeta Rajani

Technical Editor
Vrinda Amberkar

Project Coordinator
Esha Thakker

Proofreader
Aaron Nash

Indexer
Hemangini Bari

Production Coordinator
Prachali Bhiwandkar

Cover Work
Prachali Bhiwandkar

Cover Image
Sheetal Aute

Foreword

I first starting thinking about human/machine augmentations in 2000 when I started a company focused in the Telco software space. Initially, I focused on how to enable wireless content development, but at that time, devices were primitive. High speed networks hadn't fully taken on in many areas of the U.S. for mobile networks and the feeble attempts at standardization were clearly doomed. We pivoted the company to focus on speech-enabled voice applications over normal telephones.

In 2005, once again, I was intrigued by the emergence of augmenting human/machine relations by the idea of "multi-modal" applications; the concept that you could use different modes of computer input and output that are better suited for human beings. For example, I might prefer to use voice to input a question in the form of "how would I get to 123 Main Street?" to the computer. However, the results would be more realistic in the form of a visual map with turn-by-turn driving directions instead of the computer reading them back to me in voice. At that time, mobile devices had severe limitations of both processing power and memory that made it difficult to make it work for broader use. Worse, if you could build the capability, you couldn't easily distribute it to end users as the carriers owned distributions with an iron fist and each network was different and very complicated.

Steve Jobs and Apple changed all of that in 2007 with the introduction of the iPhone. Having spent a few years thinking about many great ideas that were not practical to deliver, I was immediately struck at the opportunity in front of us as human beings. The relationship of human/machine interaction at that point changed forever. The "real" personal computer was invented; that beige box under my desk was no longer the future and certainly wasn't personal anymore.

Fast forward five years and Apple's Siri is now popular and we have the ability to create amazing applications with new experiences possible within hours, not months or years. We have the ability to click on a button and make these applications available to hundreds of millions of devices on hundreds of networks all around the world almost instantly. We can create these experiences without much involvement from anyone.

Human interactions with machines will never be the same again. I once heard Eric Schmidt, Chairman of Google, say that the next two to three decades will be about machines augmenting our lives as humans, and hopefully, making them better. For the past two decades, we humans have had to keep up our machines—we run regular anti-virus software, clean the hard disk to recover lost space, and have to manage our "inbox". When's the last time you got lost in the modern world with the advent of Google Maps on your phone?

Augmented Reality is one large area of opportunity where we can digitally overlay computer augmented interactions, information, and experiences, and represent them on a real-world viewport. In the future, our human experiences will be constantly be made better and more interesting with the help of computers. Much like Google search has made the collective human brain more accessible and readily available at our finger tips, Augmented Reality is the next wave of this in a new presentation context such as phones, tablets and eventually across other types of devices such as cars and TVs.

Our mission at Appcelerator has been to enable this new wave of innovation and creative experiences by lowering the cost of development and making it more accessible to developers worldwide through Titanium.

Trevor has been a long-time friend of Appcelerator and a passionate and knowledgeable member of our community. This books explores how to use Titanium to create your own experiences to help make humanity a slightly better place than it was before.

Codestrong!

Jeff Haynie
CEO, Appcelerator

www.PacktPub.com

Support files, eBooks, discount offers and more

You might want to visit www.PacktPub.com for support files and downloads related to your book.

Did you know that Packt offers eBook versions of every book published, with PDF and ePub files available? You can upgrade to the eBook version at www.PacktPub.com and as a print book customer, you are entitled to a discount on the eBook copy. Get in touch with us at service@packtpub.com for more details.

At www.PacktPub.com, you can also read a collection of free technical articles, sign up for a range of free newsletters and receive exclusive discounts and offers on Packt books and eBooks.

www.PacktLib.PacktPub.com

Do you need instant solutions to your IT questions? PacktLib is Packt's online digital book library. Here, you can access, read and search across Packt's entire library of books.

Why Subscribe?

- ✦ Fully searchable across every book published by Packt
- ✦ Copy and paste, print and bookmark content
- ✦ On demand and accessible via web browser

Free Access for Packt account holders

If you have an account with Packt at www.PacktPub.com, you can use this to access PacktLib today and view nine entirely free books. Simply use your login credentials for immediate access.

Table of Contents

Augmented Reality using Appcelerator Titanium Starter

Welcome to Augmented Reality using Appcelerator Titanium.

Advances in technology are driven by a need. Some of the greatest advances are made during wars, the computer revolution being one of them. I doubt we will ever know the full extent of the advances made with computers during the Second World War, but they were significant. After the war ended Manchester, England became home to a team of leading academics and industry experts, where the Manchester Baby was born. This has now been replicated at the Science Museum in Manchester, and was the first fully functioning computer as we know them today.

Today a mobile phone has more processing power than these early room-size computers, but it still has limitations. Mobile devices are becoming more powerful, more usable, and more widespread. With the introduction of the iPhone, a revolution in mobile technology occurred. But mobile devices have limited processing power, storage, and memory compared to a desktop computer and this is often forgotten or ignored. When developing applications for mobile devices these considerations need to be taken into account as the applications perform badly if they aren't.

Developing an Augmented Reality application is no different. In fact more consideration has to be taken for the device it needs to run on. This type of application displays lots of data, moves it continually around the screen, and resizes components, resulting in using the device's processing power to the maximum. A lot of time and effort is spent in coding, to minimize the amount of processing required. In a lot of cases it is just too much for the device to handle cleanly.

This book explains a solution to implementing **Location-based Augmented Reality**. The solution provided has been coded using the **Appcelerator Titanium Framework** but it can be applied to most other frameworks and native solutions. It is aimed at the developers; although all the code is available and is well commented, it is not aimed at novice coders.

If you are currently implementing or thinking about Augmented Reality this book is for you. It shows a solution which works effectively, using an open source example application, **augmentedTi**. We will cover the latest Titanium APIs, coding methods, and best practices.

This book contains the following sections:

So what is Augmented Reality? – This section gives a brief overview of what Augmented Reality can be.

Installation – This section shows you how to obtain and install the augmentedTi application from bitbucket into Titanium Studio.

The application architecture – This section dives into the open source code base on the augmentedTi example application, explaining how it has been implemented.

Augmented Reality – This section explains the augmented reality solution provided within the augmentedTi application.

People and places you should get to know – This section provides you with many useful links to the project page and forums, as well as a number of helpful articles, tutorials, blogs, and the Twitter feeds of some useful people to follow.

So, what is Augmented Reality?

Augmented Reality is a term used to describe the enhancement of real-world objects or views with computer generated actions. But what does this mean?

An augmented reality application can contain various functions, be they for interaction or display. A good example of this is if you are in a museum and as you use their application, you can scan a bar code on the base of a statue and the application shows a picture of the statue with a fully interactive description. It could explain where and when it was made, who the sculpture was, and give you options to view other works by the artist. This could then be extended to show you a map of the museum highlighting different works by the artist, where they are located, and allowing you to follow the map to their locations.

Another example and the one explained in this book, is where you are at a location and you want to find different activities or venues in your proximity. This normally entails the application using the device's camera as a view and is then overlaid with icons representing items within the local area. These items can be anything from local businesses to fictitious items which just exist in cyber space. Selecting one of these items then enables interaction of varying types, the details of the premises could be displayed or a map giving you directions created.

These are just a couple of examples of the types of augmented reality applications which can be created. In reality this type of application is only limited by ideas, and the mobile device's abilities.

More information can be found on Wikipedia at `http://en.wikipedia.org/wiki/Augmented_reality`.

Installation

augmentedTi is a demonstration application, showing an implementation of Augmented Reality, using the Titanium framework.

Step 1 – What do I need?

To set up and run the augmentedTi application, you will need to have the latest version of Titanium Studio installed, a device to test on, and for iPhone an Apple developer account. The application uses Google Places to obtain its data and you will have to obtain your own API key for this feature, before getting the application from **bitbucket**.

Step 2 – Downloading Titanium Studio

If you haven't already got the latest version of Titanium, go to http://www.appcelerator.com/ and click on the download link. If you already have an Appcelerator account, log in; if not, create one (it's free). Select the version you need from the downloads area (see the following screenshot):

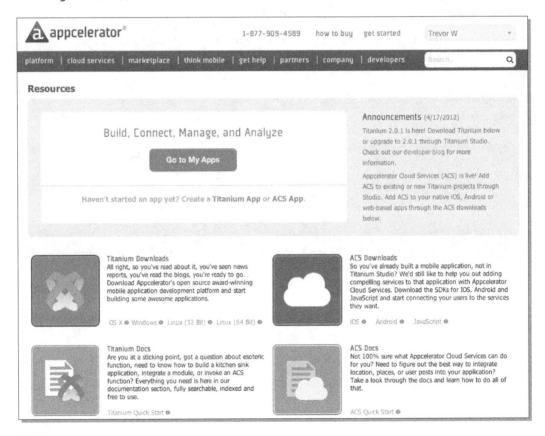

Titanium Studio is based on the Eclipse IDE, so if you are familiar with this then there should be no issues. If you are not, have a read of some of the documentation. Working with studio is outside the scope of this book. The application has been developed using Version 2.1.0 of the Titanium SDK.

Step 3 – Apple developer account

If you wish to run the application on an iPhone, you will need to configure the provisioning profile. One thing to remember is to change the application ID to meet your requirements. You can find out more about the Apple developer account at `https://developer.apple.com`.

Step 4 – Google Places API

The application uses Google Places to provide the data. You will have to use your Google account to generate the Google Places API key. Details on the API can be found at `http://code.google.com/apis/maps/documentation/places/`. Creating the API key is done at `https://code.google.com/apis/console/`.

Log in to the console using your Google account details and go to the **Services** section. About two-thirds of the way down the page you will see the **Places API** option. Switch it on. If this is your first visit to the console, an API key will be created. The API key can be found in the **API Access** section. The API key needs to be inserted into the augmentedTi application file, `services/googleFeed.js`, at the following location:

```
var apikey    =    'YOUR GOOGLE PLACES API KEY GOES HERE';
```

Step 5 – Get augmentedTi

The augmentedTi application is available from bitbucket at `https://bitbucket.org/softlywired/augmentedti` and can be imported directly into Titanium Studio.

For those who haven't done this before, open the studio and select **File** from the main menu and click on **Import**. This will bring up a selection box, as shown in the following screenshot:

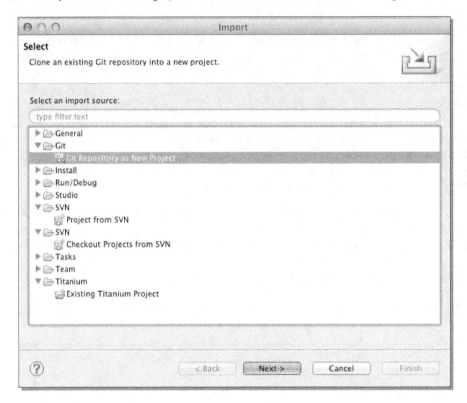

Select **Git/Git repository as New Project** and click on **Next**. This will bring up a second box, shown as follows:

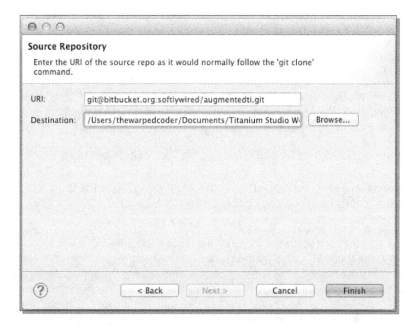

Paste the bitbucket URI, `git@bitbucket.org:softlywired/augmentedti.git`, into the **URI** box. For **Destination**, either accept the default destination or select your own and click on **Finish**.

This will import the project into the workspace and enable you to start to look around. When it is imported, open up the `tiapp.xml` file and change the application ID for your Apple provisioning profile and also insert the Google Places API key.

 You may find that you cannot run the project in the studio. This is due to a bug in Eclipse and can be remedied by deleting the project (do not delete the contents), removing the `.project` file from the source directory, and then importing it again as an existing Titanium project.

And that's it!

By this point, you should have augmentedTi installed and running on your device.

 See the README file for the latest supported platforms and devices.

The application architecture

This section dives into the open source code base of the augmentedTi example application, explaining how it has been implemented.

An overview

The augmentedTi application has been developed to demonstrate Augmented Reality in action; it has been coded using the Appcelerator Titanium Framework. This framework enables a "code once, adapt everywhere" approach to mobile application development.

It uses the commonJS architecture at its core and has a set of best practices, which can be read at `https://wiki.appcelerator.org/display/guides/Best+Practices`. The application follows these guidelines and also implements an MVC style architecture, using a controller, and event driven flow control methodology incorporating localization.

 At the current time trying to implement a CSS applied look and feel using the frameworks JSS method is not viable. The application gets around the issue of hard coding fonts, colors, and images into the application by using two files—`ui/layout.js` and `ui/images.js`. These files contain the look, feel, and images applied throughout the application, and are standalone modules, enabling them to be included in any other modules.

The application

As you start to explore the application you will see that the main bootstrap file `app.js` only contains the require of the controller file and the call to the initial function `startApp()`:

```
var ctl    =    require('/control/controller');
ctl.startApp();
```

To implement methodology for separating the code into distinct commonJS modules, the following file structure is applied:

```
i18n/en/strings.xml
resources/app.js
resources/control/controller.js
resources/images
resources/services/googleFeed.js
                  location.js
resources/tools/augmentedReality.js
            common.js
            iosBackgroundService.js
            persHandler.js
```

```
ui/images.js
    layout.js
    common/activity.js
            titleBar.js
    screens/ARScreen.js
            homeScreen.js
```

The main file which controls the application is `controller.js`. When an activity is completed, the control is returned here and the next activity is processed. This has an implication with enabling the program flow—application-level event listeners have to be added, using up resources. The application gets around this by creating a **single custom event listener**, which then calls a function to handle the flow. The fire event is handled within the `tools/common.js` file by providing a single function to be called, passing the required **type** and any other parameters:

```
Ti.App.addEventListener('GLOBALLISTENER', function(inParam){
    var gblParams    = {};
    for(var paramKeyIn in inParam) {
        if(inParam[paramKeyIn]) {
            gblParams[paramKeyIn] = inParam[paramKeyIn];
        }}
    processGlobalListener(gblParams);});

function launchEvent(inParam){
    var evtParams    = {};
    for(var paramKeyIn in inParam) {
        if(inParam[paramKeyIn]) {
            evtParams[paramKeyIn] = inParam[paramKeyIn];
        }}
    Ti.App.fireEvent('GLOBALLISTENER', evtParams);}

common.launchEvent({
    TYPE :      'ERROR',
    MESS :      'E0004'});
```

Throughout the application's commonJS modules, a standard approach is taken, defining all functions and variables as local and exporting only those required at the end of the file:

```
exports.startApp    =    startApp;
```

In keeping with the commonJS model, the modules are only required when and where they are needed. No application-level global variables are used and each part of the application is split into its own module or set of modules.

Within the application where data has to be stored, **persistent data** is used. It could have been passed around, but the amount of data is small and required across the whole application. The persistent data is controlled through the `tools/persHandler.js` module, which contains two functions—one for setting and one for getting the data. These functions accept the parameter of the record to update or return.

```
var persNames    = {
    lon :      'longitude',
    lat :      'latitude',
    width :     'screenWidth',
    height :     'screenHeight',
    bearing :      'bearing'
};

function putPersData(inParam){
    Ti.App.Properties.setString(persNames[inParam.type],
    inParam.data);

    return;}

persHandler.putPersData({
    type :      'width',
    data :      Ti.Platform.displayCaps.platformWidth
});
```

The application does not use the in-built tab navigation; instead it defines a custom title bar and onscreen buttons. This enables it to work across all platforms with the same look and feel. It also uses a custom activity indicator.

The rest of the application should be easy to follow. We will dive deeper into the Augmented Reality code in the next section.

Augmented Reality

This section explains what Augmented Reality is and the solution provided within the augmentedTi application.

With all technology something and somebody has to be first. Mobile computing and especially smart phones are still in their infancy. Resulting in new technologies, applications, and solutions being devised and applied almost daily.

Augmented Reality is only now becoming viable, as the devices, technology, and coding solutions are more advanced. In this section a coding solution is given, which shows how to implement location-based Augmented Reality. It should work on most smart phones, and can be coded in most frameworks and native code. The code examples given use the Appcelerator Titanium Framework only. No additional modules or plugins are required.

The basics

When I was creating an Augmented Reality solution, I spoke to quite a few people, searched the Web, looked at the **Appcelerator ArTi** example, and came to the conclusion that nobody was giving any real answers on how to implement a usable solution. Everybody was saying the same thing: the key is to minimize processing.

All the examples, tutorials, and documentation I found gave the same solution, which resulted in an interface that was jerky and slow.

The way it worked was quite simple in principal. The **Points of Interest** (**POIs**) were all displayed on a single screen as a series of views. These were then moved around the screen depending on the device's location and rotation. The method only showed the POIs currently in view by hiding the others.

This solution, although working, produced the effect of the POIs bouncing in and out. It also meant that every POI had to have actions taken every time the device was moved, resulting in high processing, poor performance, and a jerky interface.

The key is to minimize processing.

Over the years, computers have become ever more powerful, giving greater processing power and storage capacity. This has produced a generation of programmers, who don't have a real concept of memory and processing management. This is not a criticism; it's just a fact. They haven't had to focus on this, instead just buying more memory.

Mobile devices are different. You have a finite amount of memory and processing power available. To allow for this you need to apply different solutions. Well actually you have to go back to the birth of computing, where programmers had to think about every character they entered into their code. You don't need to minimize the code to this extent, but you will need to apply good coding practices, performance enhancements of code, and techniques to minimize processing and memory usage.

With this in mind, I started to consider how to minimize the processing of the POIs. I know I am not the first to have thought of this solution, but I may be the first to publish it.

My initial thoughts went along the lines of received suggestions; how do you avoid having to process the hidden POIs? Realizing that you would actually have almost as much processing as if you moved them, quickly negated this process.

How do you create a 360 degree panoramic view?

With this thought, I decided that's exactly what you do. You create four views, each one the same size as the device's screen. Each one representing a 90 degree view, placing the POIs on the correct view and then moving the views. This took me from moving 30-50 POIs to moving four views. This solution is generically used when displaying panoramic views of splitting the data into movable chunks.

Placing them in a view which was the width of the screen * 7, meant they could be positioned within that view and moved around easily, using the real estate off the screen, by placing the views outside of the box.

 When the code had been completed, during testing I was literally spinning on the spot and the POIs were following at the same speed. No more waiting for them to catch up, and I had set the compass change event handler to 1 degree.

Device testing

Not all mobile devices are able to run an Augmented Reality application. To ensure the application will work on the device you will need to test for certain sensors, and the camera.

The four tests which are needed to be carried out are for the following:

✦ GPS
✦ GPRS
✦ Compass
✦ Camera

Within Titanium this is relatively easy, as the framework contains APIs for such purposes. The augmentedTi code base uses four functions within the `tools/common.js` module. These return true if the sensor is available and active, or false if not.

The `controller` module calls the functions prior to loading the initial screen. The results are then displayed as blue or red blocks, enabling the application to be controlled as appropriate.

```
function checkGeoServices(){
    return (Ti.Geolocation.getLocationServicesEnabled)
    ?    true    :    false;}

function checkCompassServices(){
    return Ti.Geolocation.hasCompass;
}

function checkNetworkServices(){
    return (Titanium.Network.online)
    ?    true    :    false;
}

function checkCameraExists(){
    return (Ti.Media.isCameraSupported) ? true : false;
}
```

 We only test to see if GPRS is available. You may need to refine this test for Wi-Fi, if you have a lot of data to download.

Getting the location

The key to any location-based application is getting the device's current latitude and longitude. Augmented Reality is no exception.

The Titanium Geolocation API provides the ability to get the current location. For more information on the Titanium APIs refer to the official Appcelerator documentation at `http://developer.appcelerator.com/documentation`.

 They have recently undertaken a major revamp and update of these documents, making for an excellent resource.

Within the `services/location.js` file you will find all the functions for retrieving the device's current location. There are a couple of gotchas with initially getting the location, it doesn't always update correctly on IOS and used to causes errors on Android, but with Version 2 of Titanium Android has a new location method. To get round this we call the `retrieveCurrentPosition` function three times from the controller, putting in event handlers to make sure it is only called again when the previous call has finished.

For the location calls we need to set various values, based on the device type:

```
Ti.Geolocation.headingFilter    =    1;
Ti.Geolocation.showCalibration    =    false;

if(Ti.Platform.osname  ==  'android') {
    Ti.Geolocation.Android.accuracy =
               Ti.Geolocation.ACCURACY_HIGH;
    Ti.Geolocation.accuracy =
               Ti.Geolocation.ACCURACY_HIGH;
}
else {
    Ti.Geolocation.distanceFilter    =    10;
    Ti.Geolocation.preferredProvider    =    "gps";
    Ti.Geolocation.accuracy    =
               Ti.Geolocation.ACCURACY_NEAREST_TEN_METERS;
    Ti.Geolocation.purpose    =
               Ti.Locale.getString('gps_purpose');
}
```

We set `preferredProvider` to gps, which we can do as the device tests make sure that GPS is available and active. Although devices are only accurate to about 5 meters when getting the location, we set the best possible accuracy. The purpose is IOS-specific and is required. You will notice that we are using the localization services functionality in Titanium enabling for the application to be translated.

The main function, `retrieveCurrentPosition`, is called by the controller. This function puts the returned location details into persistent data. It uses "try-catch", enabling any errors to be handled gracefully. The controller `nextLocationCheck` function handles the calls and if the location is obtained successfully, controls the application flow to get the Google Places data. A custom activity indicator, `ui/common/activity.js`, is shown during this process. The messages are updated showing the current progress of the application.

The Titanium API `Ti.Geolocation.getCurrentPosition`, is used to obtain the current location. This is fully documented in the Appcelerator API documentation:

```
// The controller function
function nextLocationCheck(inParam){
    if(locationCount  <  2) {
```

```
            locations.retrieveCurrentPosition();
            locationCount++;
        }
        else {
            var loc     =     persHandler.retPersData({
                type :     0
            });
            var lat     =     persHandler.retPersData({
                type :     1
            });
            var mess    =     'Your current Locations is '   +
                               loc   +   '   ...  '   +   lat;
            activity.activityMessage({
                MESS :     mess
            });
            locationCount     =     0;
            retrieveGoogleFeed();
        }
    }


// The location function
function retrieveCurrentPosition(){
    try {
        var getLocation =
            Ti.Geolocation.getCurrentPosition(function(e)
        {
            if(!e.success   ||   e.error) {
                common.launchEvent({
                    TYPE :     'ERROR',
                    MESS :     'E0002'
                });
            }
            if(e.success) {
                persHandler.putPersData({
                    type :     0,
                    data :     e.coords.longitude
                });
                persHandler.putPersData({
                    type :     1,
                    data :     e.coords.latitude
                });
                common.launchEvent({
                    TYPE :     'nextLocationCheck'
```

```
                });
            }
        });
    }
    catch(err) {
        common.launchEvent({
            TYPE :      'ERROR',
            MESS :      'E0002'
        });
    }
    return;
}
```

After getting the device's current location, the application moves on to get the Google Places data.

Data processing

The application uses Google Places data to show the Augmented Reality solution in real time because it is free, well-populated, and world wide. The `services/googleFeed.js` module retrieves this data and is called from the controller. If you haven't already, you will need to create your own Google Places API key and insert it into the code where indicated. Please see the *Installation* section.

Google Places returns various data; for a lean application we only process the data we actually need. In your own application, you may have control over the data returned, enabling you to minimize this fully.

Applying the best practices and correct application architecture here is critical to getting a well-performing application. Undertaking too much processing will make the application slow and unresponsive.

In the `controller.js` file the function that processes the data is `processGoogleData`. This function loops through each record, calculates the distance and bearing from the device's location, and builds an array of the required data. It then sorts this array based on the distance. The function also updates the activity indicator screen message, and handles any errors gracefully.

If your application requires updates to the data, having built the application flow through the controller, it is simply a case of updating your location by calling the appropriate function, which will handle the remainder of the flow to build the new Augmented Reality display.

Distance and direction

There are three values that need to be calculated to be able to display the data in an Augmented Reality view. These are **distance, bearing,** and **degree**. Within the application these are calculated in the `tools/augmentedReality.js` module. A forth value, **radius,** is required to show the radar blips.

Distance

Calculating the distance between two points requires using a calculation, that you probably haven't used since school. There are three formulas commonly available to do this—**haversine, Spherical law of Cosines,** and **Pythagoras theorem**. Each has a different level of accuracy and required processing power. The haversine formula is the most accurate but also the most processor intensive.

In the augmentedTi application we use the Spherical law of Cosines formula for a few reasons. The first is that a device is only accurate to 5 meters; this formula is also accurate to about 5 meters. It requires a lot less processing power than the haversine formula. As you develop your own application, you will need to decide which is right for you, accuracy over performance is the main question.

The controller calls a function to calculate the distance passing the current latitude and longitude of the device and the data record received from Google Places. Consider the following:

```
var currLocation    = {
    lat : persHandler.retPersData({type: 1}),
    lng : persHandler.retPersData({type: 0})
};
var dataLocation    = {
    lat : inParam.DATA.results[i].geometry.location.lat,
    lng : inParam.DATA.results[i].geometry.location.lng
};
var calcDistance =    augmentedReality.calculateDistance
                      (currLocation, dataLocation);
```

The following `calculateDistance` function returns the distance between the two points:

```
function calculateDistance(point1, point2){
    var R    =    6371;
    var d    =    Math.acos(((Math.sin(point1.lat)   *
                 Math.sin(point2.lat))   +
                 (Math.cos(point1.lat)   *
                 Math.cos(point2.lat))   *
                 Math.cos(point2.lng  -  point1.lng)))   *
                 R;
    return d;
}
```

Not being a mathematician I won't be going into all the details here; suffice to say, it works, quickly and accurately enough for the augmentedTi application.

Bearing

The bearing is calculated to enable the application to show the POIs and radar blips correctly. It is also used to calculate the degree value, which is also required. The calculations for this have come from the Appcelerator example ARti application. Having already built the required longitude and latitude variables we use these again to pass to the `calculateBearing` function from the controller:

```
var calcBearing     =    augmentedReality.calculateBearing
                         (currLocation, dataLocation);
```

The `calculateBearing` function returns the bearing between the two points:

```
function calculateBearing(point1, point2){
    var lat1 =    point1.lat  *  Math.PI  /  180;
    var lat2 =    point2.lat  *  Math.PI  /  180;
    var dlng =    (point2.lng  -  point1.lng)  *
                  Math.PI  /  180;
    var y    =    Math.sin(dlng)  *  Math.cos(lat2);
    var x    =    Math.cos(lat1)  *  Math.sin(lat2)  -
                  Math.sin(lat1)  *  Math.cos(lat2)  *
                  Math.cos(dlng);
    var brng =    Math.atan2(y, x);
    return brng;}
```

Degree

The degree is calculated to enable the switch between the bearing and degrees required for displaying the POIs on the correct view. The calculations for this have again come from the Appcelerator ArTi application. To calculate the degree, we pass the previously calculated bearing to the `toDegree` function from the controller:

```
var calcDegree = augmentedReality.toDegree(calcBearing);
```

The `toDegree` function returns the degree based on the previously calculated bearing:

```
function toDegree(radius){
    return ((radius * (180 / Math.PI)) + 360) % 360;
}
```

These values are then added to the array record of the Google Places data, for use during the building of the display.

Radius

The radius is calculated by passing the bearing to the `toRadius` function. The calculation for this has again come from the Appcelerator ArTi application. It is not actually stored anywhere, as it is only required for processing the 2DMatrix, associated with the screen radar and moving the blips.

```
augmentedReality.toRadius(currBearing)
```

The `toRadius` function returns a value calculated from the previously calculated bearing:

```
function toRadius(degree)
{
    return degree  *  (Math.PI  /  180);
}
```

That is all the heavy maths. We use more while building and moving the Augmented Reality display, but they are built into the display function, which is explained shortly.

Sort

After the calculations have been performed and the data processed, we end up with an array that contains records with multiple elements:

```
googleData.push({
        id :     inParam.DATA.results[i].id,
        icon :    inParam.DATA.results[i].icon,
        name :    inParam.DATA.results[i].name,
        location :    dataLocation,
        distance :    calcDistance,
        bearing :   calcBearing,
        degree :   calcDegree,
        vicinity :    inParam.DATA.results[i].vicinity});
```

This keeps the amount of data to be passed to a minimum. The final task to perform on the data is to sort it by distance. We do this to enable the correct display of the data. During the building of the interface we process the array record by record. If we didn't sort this by distance we would have POIs that are further away on top of closer POIs. When we scale the size of the POIs while building the interface, this order of the data is essential. It avoids having to use any special calculations to work out the `zIndex`, adding to processing.

```
googleData.sort(function(aa,  bb)
        {
            return aa.distance  -  bb.distance;
        });
        googleData.reverse();
```

Building the interface

This section will go into the details of how to build the multi-view display, place the POIs on the correct view, build the radar, and display the blips.

Although this book and the example application try to show a good coding practice, for the purposes of the augmentedTi example application, I have used just one module, which incorporates the whole Augmented Reality display and movement. This could easily be split into multiple modules (and may well be in the future). This module is just over 600 lines long including comments, so it is not too excessive.

The `ui/screens/ARScreen.js` module contains the whole interface code. Now we need to see how it builds and moves the interface. When this module is called, it initially creates the new window and displays the activity indicator, making sure the user knows something is happening. It then starts to build the overlay in the `buildAROverlay` function.

The `buildAROverlay` function controls building the Augmented Reality view, which consists of the main view, the radar image, the Close button, the required Google logo, the display of the POIs, and opening the camera. Most of these are controlled by separate functions. Each specific section of the build is covered in the following subsections.

Radar

The radar is an image placed just below the top right of the screen. Its purpose is to indicate where POIs are in relation to the current direction of the device. It works by drawing blips or in this case a small view with a background color and radius to give a circle, on the image in the correct place. This is done by using the distance of the POIs from the current location and their compass bearing. We have already calculated these values in the previous sections, so we just need to apply them.

Within the augmentedTi example Augmented Reality application the Radar image is located in the `images` directory and called `radar.png`. This is an open source image found on the Web, so if you need to use it you can:

 To get get the correct radar display and movement, it is vital you know the exact size of the display area. I resolved this by having no white space around the image at all. You will also need to make the background transparent.

The radar itself is made up of two views. The first is `arRadarBck`, which is used to set the base image of the radar. The second, `arRadarImg` is used to hold the blips and rotate as the device is moved; it has a transparent background. Setting the `zIndex` guarantees that the views appear in the right layer.

The blips are generated at the same time as the POIs, to save processing the data more than once. These are built at the end of the `buildARData` function.

```
var ro      = ((images.file.radar.wCalc)  *
               (googleData[iPos].distance.toFixed(4)  /
               1000)  /  2);
var centerX = ((images.file.radar.wCalc)  /  2)  +
               (ro  *  Math.sin(googleData[iPos].bearing));
var centerY = ((images.file.radar.wCalc)  /  2)  -  (ro  *
               Math.cos(googleData[iPos].bearing));
var displayBlip  =  Ti.UI.createView({
        height :     layout.css.ar.blip.height,
        width :      layout.css.ar.blip.width,
        backgroundColor :    layout.css.ar.blip.color,
        borderRadius :    2,
        top :     centerY  -  1,
        left :    centerX  -  1,
        lat :     googleData[iPos].location.lat,
        lng :     googleData[iPos].location.lng
});
arRadarImg.add(displayBlip);
```

You will see from the code that we calculate the position using the **Distance, Bearing, Image Width** and what appears to be a random figure of **1000**. This figure is actually worked out to fit the blips onto the radar image correctly, as the distance is in kilometers. The blip is created as a view with `borderRadius` and `backgroudColor`, making a nice circle.

 These calculations have again come from the Appcelerator ArTi application.

These calculations work nicely and again, I am not a mathematician—trying to explain all the math could result in providing you with misinformation.

POIs

To display the Google Places data, or as is normally referred to as POIs, we need to build four views which will sit next to each other in a parent view and contain the POIs for the correct bearing. The `buildARDisplay` function creates these containers. The initial container is created **seven** times the screen's width and placed centrally. This gives a view which has most of it outside of the screen area. This is used to display the other four views and enable them to be easily moved around.

```
var poiDisplay =    Ti.UI.createView({
        top     :    0,
        height  :    screenHeight,
        left    :    0  -  (screenWidth  *  3),
        width   :    (screenWidth  *  7),
        backgroundColor :    'transparent',
        zIndex  :    50
    });
```

The other four views, of the same size as the screen, are then created and added to this parent view before the parent view is added to the overlay. Each of the four views is positioned by its `right` parameter. This has to be done because moving the views around, we set the right position within the parent view. If we used the left positioning, as the device is rotated, the views would move in the opposite direction to that required.

```
poiView1    =    Ti.UI.createView({
        top     :    0,
        height  :    screenHeight,
        right   :    0,
        width   :    screenWidth
    });
```

The `right` positioning is set at 0 for view 1, set at the screen width for view 2, set at twice the screen width for view 3, and 0 - the screen width for view 4.

The views are then populated with the Google Data, each view representing 90 degrees of the compass. The `buildARData` function, which we have already seen in the radar, is used to calculate which view a POI is displayed in. Each POI has a **scale** applied to it to reduce its full size down depending on the distance it is away from the device's location. As previously mentioned, the data has been sorted by distance enabling the data to be processed farthest to nearest:

```
var scale = (10 / googleData[iPos].distance).toFixed(2);
if(scale   >=   1) {
    scale   =    1.00;
}
if(scale   <=   0.35) {
    scale   =    0.35;
}
```

After the scale has been calculated the **POIs degree** value is used to select the view it is to be displayed in, calculating the `left` and `top` positions. It is built and added to that view.

 For the augmentedTi example application the Google Places icon is displayed. This keeps the data on the screen to a minimum.

In calculating the position in the view of the POI we divide the screen width by 90, and multiply it by the degree to get its exact position.

To make the application do something after the POI view has been created, the `addPOIEvent` function is called. This function adds an event listener to the image, allowing it to be pressed and display some more data on the screen.

 It is worth noting that adding event listeners within a for loop is not good practice, which is why it has been separated out into its own function.

The four views each deal with 90 degrees of the compass. View 1 has the POIs which are between 315 and 45 degrees. This is done as we require this view to be positioned "right 0" on the screen when the compass is pointing at 0 degrees. Using this as the base, the remaining views deal with the next subsequent 90 degrees, as the following code snippet shows:

```
var tmpDegCal     =     0;
var tmpView     =     null;
if (googleData[iPos].degree   <=   45   ||
   googleData[iPos].degree   >=   315) {
        tmpDegCal     =     -45;
        tmpView     =     poiView1;
}
else if (googleData[iPos].degree   <=   135) {
        tmpDegCal     =     45;
        tmpView     =     poiView2;
}
else if (googleData[iPos].degree   <=   225) {
        tmpDegCal     =     135;
        tmpView     =     poiView3;
}
else {
        tmpDegCal     =     225;
        tmpView     =     poiView4;
}
var tmpLeft = ((googleData[iPos].degree   -
            tmpDegCal)   *   (screenWidth   /   90))
            - ((layout.css.ar.detail.ics * scale) / 2);
```

```
var tmpTop      =      (screenHeight / 2)  *   scale;

if ((tmpLeft + ((layout.css.ar.detail.ics * scale / 2))) >=
        screenWidth){
            tmpLeft = screenWidth - (layout.css.ar.detail.ics *
            scale);
}
if (tmpLeft <= 0){
        tmpLeft = 0;
}
var poiItem     =      Ti.UI.createImageView({
        height :    layout.css.ar.detail.ics  *   scale,
        width :     layout.css.ar.detail.ics  *   scale,
        left :      tmpLeft,
        top :       tmpTop,
        image :     googleData[iPos].icon
});
addPOIEvent({
        VIEW :      poiItem,
        POS :       iPos
});
tmpView.add(poiItem);
tmpView      =      null;
```

This code does not deal with height, but how to apply this functionality is explained in the *Updating the Data* section.

We now have all the data built within the application and can move on to displaying it as an overlay on the camera and making it move.

The camera view

Within Titanium there are a few APIs for the media services of the device. These give straightforward ways of playing music, videos, or accessing the camera. For an Augmented Reality application, using the Ti.Media.ShowCamera API enables us to display a view through the camera, remove all the controls, and overlay our Augmented Reality data. The augmentedTi example application uses this; as we have already tested for the camera, we can either display the camera view or just add the Augmented Reality onto the window's base view.

```
if(cameraView) {
   Ti.Media.showCamera({
      success : function(event){},
      cancel : function(){},
```

```
    error : function(error){
    if(error.code  ==  Ti.Media.NO_CAMERA) {
      common.launchEvent({
        TYPE :      'ERROR',
        MESS :      'E0006'
      });
    }
    else {
      common.launchEvent({
        TYPE :      'ERROR',
        MESS :      'E0006'
      });
    }},
    mediaTypes :      [Ti.Media.MEDIA_TYPE_VIDEO,
                       Ti.Media.MEDIA_TYPE_PHOTO],
    showControls :    false,
    autohide :     false,
    autofocus :     "off",
    animated :     false,
    overlay :     arBaseView
  });
}
else {
  arWin.add(arBaseView);
}
```

This will display all the data onto the screen and make it ready to be moved around.

When the application goes into the background or the **Close** button is pressed, the camera view is removed by passing control back to the controller, and running the `resetVars` function that firstly runs `Ti.Media.hideCamera()`. It then resets the application variables, enabling the initial screen to be displayed with all the previous set values and data removed.

Moving the display

We have now hit upon the key part of Augmented Reality: making everything move as the device is rotated. Up until now we have been dealing with getting the location and data, formatting this into a usable and functional display.

 Although the method of displaying the POIs is crucial to the success of the application, it is not quite as important as getting the movement right.

As we have already seen, most Augmented Reality implementations use a very different approach to the solution in this book. If we had written the normal solution I would now be explaining how to minimize the movement of 20 - 50 POIs and only access the ones currently in view. But we didn't. We created four views and positioned the POIs in these, making the movement of the views straightforward.

We start by activating the **Compass** and setting its "heading change" event to 1 degree. For this we return to the `services/location.js` module. Again it is all controlled by the `Ti.Geolocation` API:

```
Ti.Geolocation.headingFilter    =    1;
Ti.Geolocation.showCalibration   =    false;
```

We have an initial function, `retrieveCurrentDirection`, which gets the initial compass magnetic heading. Using try-catch enables us to handle errors gracefully. The `headingCallback` function is fired when the **Compass Sensor** is updated by 1 degree. This is triggered by the `heading` event listener, which is added in its own function:

```
function retrieveCurrentDirection(){
    var geoLocFuncVar =
        Ti.Geolocation.getCurrentHeading(function(e){
        if(e.error) {
            common.launchEvent({
                TYPE :      'ERROR',
                MESS :      'E0005'
            });
        }
        try {
            addDirectionHandlerLocal();
        }
        catch(err) {
            common.launchEvent({
                TYPE :      'ERROR',
                MESS :      'E0005'
            });
        }
        persHandler.putPersData({
            type :     4,
            data :     e.heading.magneticHeading
        });
    });
}
function headingCallback(e){
    if(e.error) {
        common.launchEvent({
```

```
            TYPE :      'ERROR',
            MESS :      'E0005'
        });
    }
    else {
        persHandler.putPersData({
            type :      4,
            data :      e.heading.magneticHeading
        });
        common.launchEvent({
            TYPE :      'rotateDisplay'
        });
    }
}
```

The gotcha with the compass is on the event listener. If we try to add it when it is already active, it can produce weird results. Trying to remove it when it isn't added can crash the application. Also, if we leave it active when the application closes or goes into the background, it uses up the device's resources and re-opening the app can cause it to crash.

We can resolve these issues with two other functions—one which adds the event listener and one which removes it. We have a module variable set to make sure we only add or remove it where required.

```
function removeDirectionHandlerLocal(){
    if(compassEventSet) {
        Ti.Geolocation.removeEventListener('heading',
        headingCallback);
        compassEventSet     =     false;
    }
}
function addDirectionHandlerLocal(){
    if(!compassEventSet) {
        Ti.Geolocation.addEventListener('heading',
        headingCallback);
        compassEventSet     =     true;
    }
}
```

The function to add the event listener is called from the `retrieveCurrentHeading` function, which is called from the `controller`. To make sure that we do not leave the event listener functioning, when the Augmented Reality view or the application is closed then the `controller` calls the `removeDirectionHandler` function and if the event handler is active it removes it.

Having the compass updating via the `heading` event, we now need to move the display. This is done by using the `rotateDisplay` function within `ARScreen.js`, which is called from `controller`, and triggered by the compass heading event.

`rotateDisplay` receives the bearing and checks to see what it is. It calculates the position of the primary view displayed on the screen and positions the other views relative to this, using a flag that is set at the start of the movement and unset at the end.

This makes sure that the movement is only occurring at a single time. You will see that we use the current bearing minus the bearing offset multiplied by the screen width, which is divided by 90 to calculate the `right` position of the main view. Also, the main view is different depending on the current bearing.

 It may seem straightforward, but it is critical that this is applied correctly. This short piece of code is the whole key to making the Augmented Reality application function.

Before removing the flag, we rotate the blips on the radar, by applying a 2DMatrix to the view, which contains the blips. The reason we have the view on the radar containing the blips is purely because if we added the blips to the view containing the radar image, the whole image would be rotated, which is not what is required. This is where we use the `toRadius` function to calculate the rotation required.

```
function rotateDisplay(){
  if(!rotateFlag) {
    rotateFlag = true;
    var currBearing = parseInt(persHandler.retPersData({
                         type :    4
                         }), 10);
    if(currBearing  <=  90) {
      poiView1.right = ((currBearing  -  0)  *
      (screenWidth  /  90))  +  (screenWidth  *  3);
      poiView2.right = poiView1.right  -  screenWidth;
      poiView3.right = poiView2.right  -  screenWidth;
      poiView4.right = poiView1.right  +  screenWidth;
    }
    else if(currBearing  <=  180) {
      poiView2.right = ((currBearing  -  90)  *
      (screenWidth  /  90))  +  (screenWidth  *  3);
      poiView3.right = poiView2.right  -  screenWidth;
      poiView4.right = poiView3.right  -  screenWidth;
      poiView1.right = poiView2.right  +  screenWidth;
    }
    else if(currBearing  <=  270) {
      poiView3.right     =      ((currBearing  -  180)  *
```

```
        (screenWidth / 90)) + (screenWidth * 3);
        poiView4.right = poiView3.right - screenWidth;
        poiView1.right = poiView4.right - screenWidth;
        poiView2.right = poiView3.right + screenWidth;
    }
    else {
        poiView4.right = ((currBearing - 270) *
        (screenWidth / 90)) + (screenWidth * 3);
        poiView1.right = poiView4.right - screenWidth;
        poiView2.right = poiView1.right - screenWidth;
        poiView3.right = poiView4.right + screenWidth;
    }
    arRadarImg.transform = Ti.UI.create2DMatrix().rotate(-
augmentedReality.toDegree(augmentedReality.toRadius(currBearing)));

    removeFlag();
  }
}
```

These were the key details of how the augmentedTi example Augmented Reality application was built, giving the details of the solution applied. The scope of the requirements of this project have now been met, but there are a couple of items worth covering, which you will probably need. These are covered in the following sections and explain how to update the data as the device moves. I am sure that in the near future the open source code will be updated to include these items.

Updating the data

Up to now we have seen how to create what I like to term *A Single Plain of Existence*, which is where the data remains static and moves across the screen, without consideration for the location movement of the device or the tilt. This section covers how to implement the **height, distance**, and **data** to the code base.

Height

Having POIs at different heights enables an interesting user experience as you can set a POI on the top of a building or directly on the ground, making the user tilt their device to show the information. To accomplish this, the data for the application needs to have a height value. Currently, Google Places doesn't have this value, which is why it isn't included here.

When you have a height value you can manipulate the tilt movement of the device by using the `Ti.Accelerometer` API. This gives you the ability to find the tilt and adjust the four views, by increasing their initial height to what you require. As an example you can double the height, making the bottom o feet and the top 50 feet. Then each view would be able to be adjusted on the screen within the move section by the current `accelerometer` value.

Distance

As the device moves closer to a POI, it is nice to give the illusion that the POI is getting closer. To achieve this effect a new function to update the location is required. This would listen for a location update and do something when the device has moved say, by 10 meters.

For this you would set the `Ti.Geolocation.distance` parameter and add a `location` event listener, creating a `locationCallBack` function, which triggers another function that resizes the POIs based on distance. The method to resize the POIs is the same as the one used to size them originally.

The gotcha though is that you have to loop through all the POIs view components, calculate the distance based on the new coordinates, and resize the height and width given the new scale, on the original image size.

 Run this only as a single instance and not when the view movement is occurring. Make sure that you have a flag set to only allow it to be run in this manner.

When this is done, consideration also needs to be made for the POIs suddenly being behind the device instead of in front. This means that the process of updating the POIs across views needs to be applied.

 The advantage with this solution is that although a lot more processing is undertaken, it still only affects the POIs in view as far as the user is concerned and the display is easily made to appear to the user, clean and smooth.

Data

The augmentedTi example application only updates the Google Places data when you go back to the initial screen. It is quite an easy task to update the data every 100 meters, by applying the `location` event listener and having a count to 10. When updating the data, you would want to put the activity indicator on the screen and remove the event listeners until the data is fully updated. This is effectively the same as going back to the initial screen and starting the process from getting the data.

Another method could be to build a second set of four views with the new data on and then replace the original views with these. It would negate the need to show the user that the application is processing new data and enable a smooth transition.

If you have followed everything mentioned till now, you should now have an application on your device whose opening screen looks as follows:

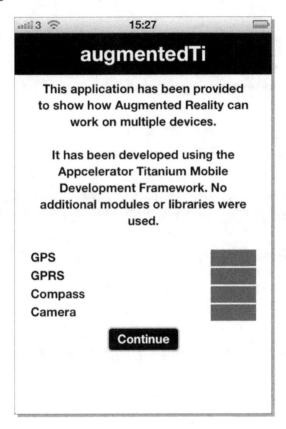

People and places you should get to know

If you need help with Augmented Reality using Appcelerator Titanium, here are some people and places it's worth getting familiar with.

Official sites

Appcelerator has some very useful resources for coding using their Titanium framework:

+ **Homepage**: `www.appcelerator.com`
+ **Manual and documentation**: `docs.appcelerator.com`
+ **Wiki**: `wiki.appcelerator.org`
+ **Blog**: `developer.appcelerator.com/blog`

Articles and tutorials

The best place to follow anything on Augmented Reality is `http://www.augmentedadvertising.com/`. This site has lots of information and links to the most relevant articles, books, and applications.

As Titanium becomes more commonplace, more training materials, reference guides, and community forums are appearing. But the only real place to get the latest information at the time of writing this book is `www.appcelerator.com`.

Twitter

Some useful people to follow on Twitter regarding Augmented Reality and Titanium are the following:

+ `http://twitter.com/#!/AugmentedAdvert`
+ `http://twitter.com/#!/appcelerator`
+ `http://twitter.com/#!/learningTI`
+ `http://twitter.com/#!/AppC_QA`
+ `http://twitter.com/#!/jHaynie`
+ `http://twitter.com/#!/softlywired`
+ Follow the author at `http://twitter.com/#!/thewarpedcoder`

Book links

+ http://www.appcelerator.com/

+ https://developer.apple.com

+ http://code.google.com/apis/maps/documentation/places/

+ https://code.google.com/apis/console/

+ https://bitbucket.org/softlywired/augmentedti

+ https://wiki.appcelerator.org/display/guides/Best+Practices

+ http://developer.appcelerator.com/documentation

+ For more Open Source information, follow Packt at http://twitter.com/#!/packtopensource

Index

About the author

Trevor Ward has been developing business applications for over 20 years. Starting as a Cobol Developer, he has worked on various large scale projects that included the Y2K issues. Moving into web development in the late 90s using Perl, HTML, JavaScript, and Oracle, he was a part of the team that developed internal business applications for Jaguar cars.

After moving on, he was able to update his skills for Ruby on Rails and Adobe Flex, before 18 months ago picking up on the mobile development platform. He uses Titanium exclusively for mobile development and is an Appcelerator Titan (community expert), TCAD and TCE qualified, and spends as much time as possible, answering questions on the forums.

About the reviewers

Ben Bahrenburg is an Appcelerator Titanium Titan, TCAD qualified, and frequent speaker on mobile development strategies. Ben specializes in building enterprise solutions using Mobile Technologies, Geo Location Services, and Domain-specific Languages. Over the last decade he has provided mobility solutions for numerous Fortune 100 organizations. He spends much of his time blogging about mobile development and creating open source Titanium modules for the community.

Imraan Jhetam is a medical doctor and entrepreneur living in England with equal love for both Medical Law and Technology. He earned his medical degree from the University of Natal in 1983, his MBA from the University of Witwatersrand, and a Masters of Law degree from Cardiff University.

Imraan has been fascinated by computers since his youth and taught himself the basics of programming during his university years. He has been writing programs since the mid 70s in various languages and for different platforms, and has fond memories of his first Apple IIe with its then impressive 64 KB RAM.

When he is not busy seeing patients or writing medico-legal reports, he spends his time developing applications. He has developed Snappa, a social sharing game that is the better way to draw something for friends. This was written using the incredible Titanium Studio tools and Appcelerator Cloud Services and is now in the Apple and Android App Stores. He was also third prize winner at the first Codestrong Hackathon with two e-payment apps—PayBill and PayPad, which also included social media, geo-location, photos, and bar-codes. These were developed in a restricted and short time using Appcelerator Titanium Studio.

You can contact Imraan via `www.snappa.mobi` or via Twitter `@The__i`.

Thank you for buying
Augmented Reality using Appcelerator Titanium Starter

About Packt Publishing

Packt, pronounced 'packed', published its first book "*Mastering phpMyAdmin for Effective MySQL Management*" in April 2004 and subsequently continued to specialize in publishing highly focused books on specific technologies and solutions.

Our books and publications share the experiences of your fellow IT professionals in adapting and customizing today's systems, applications, and frameworks. Our solution based books give you the knowledge and power to customize the software and technologies you're using to get the job done. Packt books are more specific and less general than the IT books you have seen in the past. Our unique business model allows us to bring you more focused information, giving you more of what you need to know, and less of what you don't.

Packt is a modern, yet unique publishing company, which focuses on producing quality, cutting-edge books for communities of developers, administrators, and newbies alike. For more information, please visit our website: www.packtpub.com.

Writing for Packt

We welcome all inquiries from people who are interested in authoring. Book proposals should be sent to author@packtpub.com. If your book idea is still at an early stage and you would like to discuss it first before writing a formal book proposal, contact us; one of our commissioning editors will get in touch with you.

We're not just looking for published authors; if you have strong technical skills but no writing experience, our experienced editors can help you develop a writing career, or simply get some additional reward for your expertise.

Appcelerator Titanium Smartphone App Development Cookbook

ISBN: 978-1-84951-396-8   Paperback: 308 pages

Over 80 recipes for creating native mobile applications specifically for iPhone and Andriod smartphones - no Objective-C or Java required

1. Leverage your JavaScript skills to write mobile applications using Titanium Studio tools with the native advantage!

2. Extend the Titanium platform with your own native modules

3. A practical guide for packaging and submitting your apps to both the iTunes store and Android Marketplace

Processing 2: Creative Programming Cookbook

ISBN: 978-1-84951-794-2   Paperback: 306 pages

Over 90 highly-effective recipes to unleash your creativity with interactive art, graphics, computer vision, 3D, and more

1. Explore the Processing language with a broad range of practical recipes for computational art and graphics

2. Wide coverage of topics including interactive art, computer vision, visualization, drawing in 3D, and much more with Processing

3. Create interactive art installations and learn to export your artwork for print, screen, Internet, and mobile devices

Please check **www.PacktPub.com** for information on our titles

www.ingramcontent.com/pod-product-compliance
Lightning Source LLC
LaVergne TN
LVHW080105070326
832902LV00014B/2443